TopReaders

The Great Wall of China

Denise Ryan

Contents

The Great Wall of China
is the longest structure
ever built. Let's find out
who built it and why!

Before the Wall

People have lived in China for many thousands of years.

About 3,500 years ago,
Chinese people made metal pots.

People at War

Sometimes, Chinese people attacked the rulers. They wanted to rule China themselves.

These fierce warriors attacked on horses.

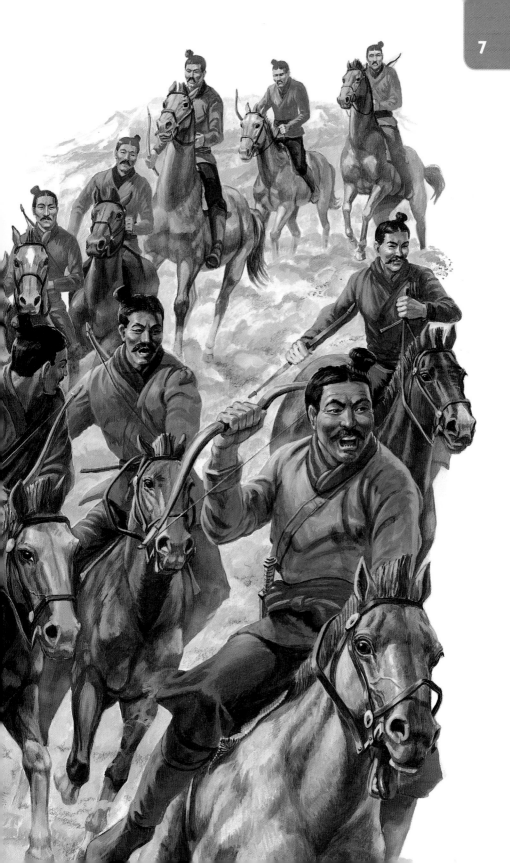

Invaders

People from outside China also attacked the Chinese rulers. Many came from the north.

sword

These invaders used arrows and swords to attack China.

arrow

The First Emperor

Qin, the first emperor of China, helped stop the wars by building the Great Wall of China.

Emperor Qin

Thousands of
life-size pottery
warriors and horses
were buried in
Emperor Qin's tomb.

Building the Wall

Millions of workers built the Great Wall. The wall is made from rocks, mud, soil, and bricks.

Qin's wall took workers more than 10 years to build.

Defending the Wall

Soldiers lived and worked along the wall. From the watchtowers, they could see if invaders were coming.

This soldier is shooting an arrow to stop an invader.

watchtower

Trade and Travel

The Great Wall stretches across the plains and mountains of northern China.

Great Wall

trader

Traders traveled safely inside the wall.

Behind the Wall

The ancient Chinese were safe from attack because they were protected by the wall.

Today's Great Wall

Today, some parts of the wall are well cared for. Other parts of it are falling down.

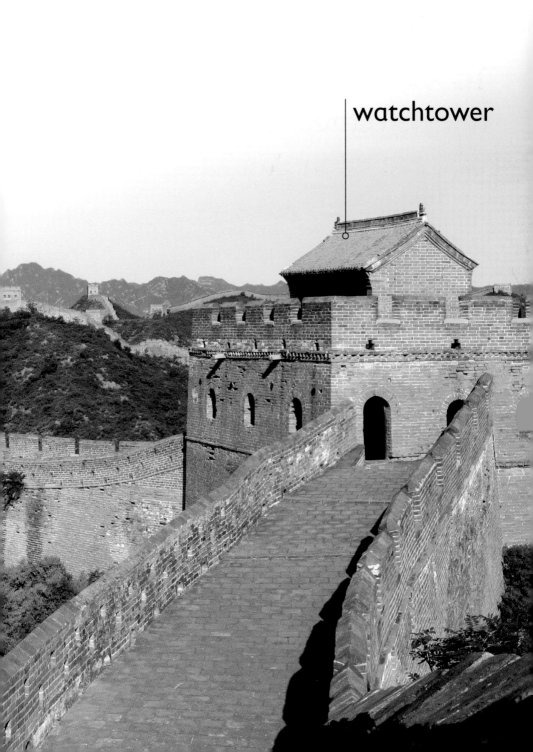

watchtower

Visitors

Thousands of tourists visit the Great Wall of China every year.

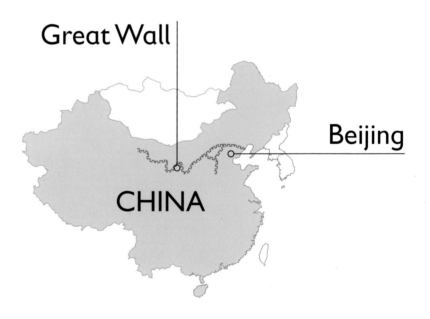

Great Wall

Beijing

CHINA

Most people visit the wall near the city of Beijing.

Quiz

Can you match each picture with its name?

emperor   invader

soldier   Great Wall